Caribbean/Soul Food Cookbook

A Collection of Favorite Recipes Including Jerk

Lincoln Allen

authorHOUSE®

AuthorHouse™
1663 Liberty Drive
Bloomington, IN 47403
www.authorhouse.com
Phone: 1-800-839-8640

© 2010 Lincoln Allen. All rights reserved.

No part of this book may be reproduced, stored in a retrieval system, or transmitted by any means without the written permission of the author.

First published by AuthorHouse   4/8/2010

ISBN: 978-1-4520-0830-1 (e)
ISBN: 978-1-4520-0829-5 (sc)

Printed in the United States of America
Bloomington, Indiana

This book is printed on acid-free paper.

CONTENTS

FOREWORD	vii
READING THE RECIPE	viii
SOUPS	1
SALADS	15
PORK & BEEF	21
POULTRY	27
GOAT/MUTTON	37
FISH	40
DRESSINGS & SAUCES	59
ROTI/PATTIES	66
VEGETABLES	72
DESSERTS	79
CAKES & BREADS	88
CEREALS	119
DRINKS	123
PRESERVES	138
TOFFEE	153
GLOSSARY OF COOKING TERMS	157
USEFUL COOKING AND HOUSEHOLD HINTS	161
OVEN TEMPERATURE GUIDE	164
TABLE OF MEASUREMENTSAND	166
MISCELLANEOUS EQUIVALENTS	166
METRIC CONVERSION CHART	168

FOREWORD

I have particularly enjoyed planning this Soul Food Cook Book because I know how much cooks will appreciate every recipe.

We have tried to include varied selections of dishes. Some are plain and traditional; all have been proven to be excellent.

Also included are helpful hints and recipes for entertaining and much more. It may surprise you to find that you will have no difficulty in preparing these dishes that seem elaborate.

In this book, even the most complicated recipes are written with clarity and in such detail as to be within the capabilities of both beginners and experienced cooks. However, test out any of these and you will agree that they are not only successful, but delicious, quick and easy to prepare.

READING THE RECIPE

Before you cook, read your recipe and make sure that you understand it. Look up any term you are not familiar with. Make sure that you have all the ingredients and lay them out on the table. Turn on your oven and set it at the required heat. Wash your fruit or vegetables.

Prepare any meat and cover until ready for use. It is not good to use foods directly from the refrigerator, except of course, when making pastry. Take out your baking pan, dust it (it should be clean when put away) and line or grease it as the recipe requires. Lay out your utensils, wash your hands and you are ready to begin.

SOUPS

CLEAR TURTLE SOUP

　　3 lbs. turtle meat
　　3 qts. water
　　3 diced carrots
　　2 diced onions
　　* salt & thyme - 6 pimento grains
　　* lime peel - pinch of sage
　　* sherry to taste

Set all ingredients except lime peel and sage to boil for about 3 hours. One hour before straining, add a piece of lime peel and some sage. Strain through a fine sieve. Add some sherry and pieces of turtle meat when serving.

BEET SOUP

8 large cooked and peeled beets
1 lb. soup meat cut into cubes
3 diced tomatoes
2 qts. water
1 cup shredded cabbage
* salt & pepper
* sour cream

Combine meat, tomatoes and water in a saucepan. Bring to a boil. Skim and cook for about an hour. Add the cabbage, salt and pepper. Cook for 30 minutes. Grate the beetroots and add to the soup with salt and pepper. Cook for 15 minutes.

Serve very hot, with a spoonful of sour cream and a few pieces of the meat in each soup bowl.

SEA WEED SOUP

Irish Moss

2 cups chicken broth
1 chopped onion
1 beaten egg
1 cup washed sea weed
* salt & pepper

Mix chicken broth, onion, sea weed and seasonings. Bring to a boil and simmer for about 20 minutes. Remove the sea weed and add the beaten egg to the broth when it is cool. Reheat to serve, but do not boil.

FISH TEA

Soup

3 lbs. fish cut into pieces
6 cups water
2 chopped onions
2 chopped tomatoes
1 hot pepper
1 tsp. thyme
* squeeze of lime juice

Place all ingredients in a pot with water. Bring to a boil, then simmer gently for about an hour. Strain off liquid and serve with chopped parsley.

PUMPKIN SOUP

1 lb. pumpkin
1/2 lb. pig's tail
1 small onion
2 small cocoa
1 bunch leggins (soup seasoning)
2 tsp. salt
1 small hot pepper
3 pints water
1 chocho

Wash and peel pumpkin, cocoas, chocho, cut into thin cubes, prepare seasoning and meat (soak pig's tail if very salty). Put water, vegetables, pig's tail and seasoning in a covered pot to cook. Simmer until vegetables are thoroughly broken down. Stir with wooden spoon and colander. Add dumplings if liked. Serve very hot.

SPLIT PEA SOUP

1 cup split peas
3 pints cold water
1/4 lb. salt pork thinly sliced
1 ham knuckle, if procurable
1/2 lb. salt beef
1 lb. corned pork
2 chopped onions
* pepper
1/2 cup cream or evaporated milk

Soak peas overnight. Pour off water and pick out black grain. Put with water and simmer for 2 hours. Add the meat and simmer another 2 hours. Remove meat and pass peas and liquid through a colander. Put back to boil for another hour with onions and pepper seasoning. Cream or evaporated milk just before serving will greatly improve the soup. The secret for a good split pea soup is very long simmering. When you think it is done, give it another hour.

PEANUT SOUP

    1 cup peanuts
    1 qt. milk
    2 Tbsp. butter
    2 Tbsp. flour
    * salt & pepper

Cook peanuts until soft. Remove skins, mash or grind until very fine. Let milk come to a boil. Add peanuts and milk, stir in flour. Season with salt and pepper to taste. Serve hot.

GANGOOR RED PEA SOUP

1 pint peas (soaked overnight)
2 qts. water
1 lb. soup meat
1 sliced cocoa
1 chopped onion
* thyme, salt & pepper

Boil peas with soup meat in water until tender. Remove the meat and put peas through a colander, rub out and discard skin. Place liquid on stove with seasonings and cocoa. Add more water if necessary. When cocoa is cooked and dissolved, the soup is reedy. Bits of boiled meat can be added.

TRIPE SOUP

    4 lbs. tripe
    1 pair pig's trotters
    1/2 cup vinegar
    4 qts. water
    2 chopped onions
    2 diced potatoes
    2 cups diced chochos
    * salt & pepper

Soak tripe and trotters in vinegar and water to cover for 2 hours. Drain and rinse. Place tripe, trotters and water in a pot. Bring to a boil and skim. Cook over low heat for about 3 hours. Strain off the liquid. Cut tripe into small pieces and set aside. Discard trotters. Using about 6 cups of the liquid, add seasonings and vegetables. Cook for about 1/2 hour. Add the trip and simmer for a further 10 minutes. Correct seasoning. This is a thick soup.

OKRA SOUP

3/4 lb. salt beef
1 qt. water
1 doz. okras
Indian Kale or callaloo
*salt & pepper
* tomatoes, escallion, thyme, red pepper

Wash beef and soak overnight. Cut up okras and put in water along with the beef and simmer gently for about 2 hours. Chop fine some kale or callaloo and add to the soup. Simmer, add seasoning. The soup may be strained before serving.

COW HEEL SOUP

    1 pair cow heels
    6 cups water
    1 chopped onion
    1 diced chocho
    1 diced carrot
    1 chopped cocoa
    1 hot pepper
    2 tsp. salt
    * squeeze of lime juice
    * parsley

    Wash cow heels in lime juice. Cut up and boil in salted water. Skim frequently. Cook 2-3 hours over low heat. Add vegetables and seasonings. Boil until vegetables are tender. Serve with chopped parsley or plain rice.

MUTTON SOUP

3 breakfast cupful cold water
1/2 lb. mutton
1 Tbsp. rice
* salt to taste
Block of carrot and turnip
spoonful chopped parsley

Place water in pan and bring to the boil. Wipe meat and place in the boiling water; add salt and cook slowly for half an hour. Wash the rice and add it; cook for 1 hour longer. If desired, some blocks of vegetables may be added with the rice and chopped parsley. Place meat on a hot plate, put the vegetables on the side and serve the soup separately.

PEPPER POT

2 lbs. chopped calaloo or spinach
2 qts. water
1 lb. soup meat
2 slices bacon or a pig's tail
1 lb. precooked shrimp
1 doz. okras sliced
1 minced onion
1 diced cocoa
*salt, pepper, herbs, hot pepper to taste

Place meat and bacon in a soup pot with water. Boil until meat is tender. Add calaloo, okras, cocoa and seasonings. Simmer until soup has thickened. Remove hot pepper and meat (or may be left in if desired). Small flour dumplings (optional) and the shrimps are added. Simmer 15 minutes longer.

SALADS

ACKEE SALAD

2 cups boiled ackees
2 chopped hard boiled eggs
* a few strips of cooked chicken

Prepare ackees and boil for 1 minute. Turn into a colander and run cold water over the ackees, which must be firm. Mix with chopped hard boiled eggs and strips of chicken. Season to taste.

TROPICAL SPLENDER

Fruit Salad

1 ripe bananas
2 oranges
2 grapefruits
1 large sliced pan pan
1 sliced (medium) melon
4 tangerines
1 large mango
1 doz. garden cherries
6 oz. sugar
* food colouring
1/2 pint water

Boil sugar and water together to form a thin syrup, set aside to cool. Wash peel and cut fruits into cubes. Mix fruits together in a dish. Pour syrup onto fruit, add fruit colouring, chill before serving. Serves 6 people.

SOULFUL SALAD

1 cup freshly grated coconut
2 cups finely shredded cabbage
1 cup pineapple cubes
1 cup mayonnaise
* lettuce leaves

Combine coconut, cabbage and pineapple with mayonnaise mixing well. Chill and serve on lettuce leaves.

LOBSTER SALAD

* shredded lettuce
* lobster meat
* dressing
1 cup mayonnaise
1 dessert spoon creole sauce
1 tsp. onion powder
* a few drops of lime juice

For each person, arrange shredded lettuce on a plate. Top with a helping of lobster meat which has been tossed with the dressing below. Decorate with olives and strips of celery.

AFRICAN SALAD

2 oranges
1/4 cup pitted black olives
2 onions
? olive oil
1/4 tsp. sugar
1/4 tsp. salt

Thinly slice oranges, onions and olives. Mix together olive oil, salt and sugar and toss with salad. Serve individually in cups of iceberg lettuce. Serves 4.

PORK & BEEF

ROAST PORK

3 lb. loin of pork, with skin intact
oil, salt, flour

For the gravy:
2 tsp. flour
1/2 pint well-flavored stock

To serve:
Small bunch of watercress

1. Set the oven at 400F, gas mark 6.
2. Score the rind (cracking skin) with a sharp knife in cuts about 1/4" apart cutting through the skin, but not right through the fat. Place in roasting pan..
3. Brush skin with oil, sprinkle with salt & flour to help give crisp cracking.
4. Place in oven for 1 hour, 40 minutes (25 minutes per pound, plus 25 minutes extra).
5. Once the pork is cooked, turn off the oven. Place the roast on a serving dish and put it back into the oven, leaving the door ajar if it is still very hot.
6. Tip all but a dessert spoonful of fat from the roasting pan, reserving as much of the meat juices as possible.
7. Add the flour and mix over the heat until well browned.
8. Remove from heat, add the stock and mix well with wire whisk or wooden spoon. Return to the heat and bring slowly up to the boil, whisking all the time. Simmer for a few minutes until gravy is shiny. Season with salt and fresh ground black pepper to taste. Strain into a warmed gravy boat.
9. Garnish the pork with a bunch of watercress and serve with gravy and apple sauce.

JERK PORK

2 oz. freshly roasted pimento berries
6 stalks of scallions
4 cinammon leaves
2-3 hot peppers chopped
1 Tbsp. grated nutmet
* salt *& pepper to taste
3-5 lbs. pork chops or loin

Chop pimento berries finely. Add finely chopped scallions, cinammon leaves and hot petters and blend to a paste. Spread paste over pork. Rub in seasonings and leave to marinate for ½-1 hour.

Barbeque meat over slow charcoal fire, preferably made from pimento wood. Serve with hard dough bread. or rice.

PORK CHOPS WITH PINEAPPLE

4 chops
1 cup pineapple chunks
8 prunes or 1 cup raisins
1 tsp. grated lime peel
* sprinkle with sugar and salt
* bread crumbs
* a lump of butter
2 cups shredded cabbage
* salt
1/4 cup vinegar
1 Tbsp. water

Brown chops and sprinkle with salt. Place one on top of the other in a casserole in layers with the pineapple, prunes, peel and sugar. Cover with bread crumbs and dot with butter. Bake in a slow oven 300F for 1 1/2 hours. Serve with shredded cabbage which has been sprinkled with salt and boiled in vinegar and water. When tender, strain and serve hot.

BEEF CURRY WITH GREEN BANANAS

3 green bananas, peeled & cut in 1/4" slices
1 1/2 lb. stewing beef
3 Tbsp. oil
2 Tbsp. curry powder
2 onions
1 12 Tbsp. flour
1/4 cup tomato ketchup
1/2 tsp. salt
1/2 cup rum

Boil bananas in salted water for 20 minutes. Drain and reserve. Cut beef into cubes and brown in oil. Transfer to a saucepan. Add sliced onions. Stir in flour, salt and tomato ketchup and cook for 5 minutes. Cover with curry powder mixed in some water. Stir and simmer for 1/2 hour. Add rum and green banana slices. Heat through.

STUFFED PEPPERS

Beef

12 medium sized sweet green peppers
2 1/2 oz. rice
1 onion, chopped
salt & pepper
4 Tbsp. wine vinegar
2 cups (generous) tomato juice
1 lb. minced beef
1 small clove garlic, crushed
1 Tbsp. chicken soup powder (optional)
3 Tbsp. sugar
water

Cut off the tops of the peppers and take out the seeds. Mix the beef, rice, garlic, onion, salt & pepper and pack into each pepper to no more than two-thirds and then replace the tops. Fit the peppers together closely into a saucepan. Mix the soup powder, vinegar, sugar and tomato juice, and add enough water to just cover the peppers. Bring to a boil and then reduce the heat and cook for about 1 hour until the peppers are tender and about two-thirds of the liquid is absorbed. For a difference, you can add a grated carrot to the meat mixture. The flavour of the sauce can also be altered by the addition of garlic or honey. Serves 6 to 8.

POULTRY

BARBECUED CHICKEN WITH SPECIAL SAUCE

    1 3 lb. chicken
    1 cup tomato sauce or ketchup
    1 tsp. creole sauce
    2 Tbsp. vinegar
    1 tsp. dry mustard
    1 tsp. sugar
* a drop or two or hot sauce

Cut chicken into pieces. Season with salt & pepper and grill over hot coals basting frequently with sauce made by combining last six ingredients and bringing them to a boil.

DUNK CHICKEN

2 lbs. chicken cut in pieces
2 qts. water
1 tsp. salt
* sherry or rum or white wine

    Heat to boiling, 2 qts. of water, salt and chicken. Cover and simmer for about 5 minutes. Place chicken in a bowl or jar and cover completely with liquor. Keep refrigerated for 1 week. Serve cold.

LEMON CHICKEN

2 whole chicken breasts
1 lemon, peeled and seeded
1/2 slice dry white bread
2 Tbsp. sour cream or evaporated milk
2 Tbsp. sherry
* Worcestershire sauce
* salt, pepper, paprika

Split chicken breasts, discard skin and bones. Whirl lemon, bread, sherry, sour cream, sherry, Worcestershire sauce, salt and pepper in blender. Arrange chicken breasts in 8-inch square baking dish. Top with lemon mixture, sprinkle with paprika. Cook for 10 minutes, rotating dish one-half turn every 2 minutes until chicken is tender and juices run clear when pierced with a fork. Let stand 5 minutes before serving. Serves 6.

GLAZED TURKEY ROAST

2(12-16 oz.) turkey drumsticks, thawed if frozen
Salt & pepper
1/2 cup jam
2 Tbsp. sherry or water
1 tsp. Worcestershire sauce

Preheat toaster-oven to 450F. Sprinkle drumsticks with salt and pepper. Place on oven pan and set on rack of toaster-oven. Bake 30 minutes, turning halfway through cooking time. Reduce heat to 375F. Bake 1 hour longer, turning halfway through cooking time. Meanwhile, combine jam or spread, sherry and Worcestershire sauce in small bowl. At end of baking time, spread 1/4 of mixture on each drumstick. Bake 10 minutes. Turn drumsticks and spread remaining glaze. Bake 10 minutes longer until turkey is fork tender.

TURKEY GRAVY

1 cup drippings from roast (or drippings and water to measure 1 cup)
2 Tbsp. cold water
1 Tbsp. cornstarch
1/4 tsp. salt
Dash pepper

Pour drippings into small saucepan and cook over medium heat. In cup, combine cornstarch and water until smooth. Gradually, stir into saucepan and heat to boiling. Stir constantly. Boil gravy 2 minutes or until thickened. Stir in salt and pepper. Yield about 1 cup gravy.

TURKEY WITH CORNBREAD STUFFING

12 lb. turkey
3 Tbsp. butter or margarine
2 cups sliced mushrooms
1/2 cup chopped onion
1 cup chopped celery
1/2 cup chopped green pepper
1/2 tsp. rubbed sage
30 oz. turkey gravy, divided
16 oz. cornbread stuffing mix

In large heavy pan, over medium heat, brown mushrooms, onions, celery, green peppers and sage in butter until vegetables or tender. Add 1 can gravy and stuffing mix. Mix until well blended.

Rinse the cavity of turkey and pat dry. Lightly spoon stuffing into large cavity. Secure opening by placing skewers across it and lacing shut with cord. Stuff wish bone cavity lightly. Skewer neck skin. Heat oven to 325F. Loosely cover turkey with foil. Place in oven and cook for 4 to 4 1/2 hours. Baste occasionally. Spoon remaining stuffing into buttered 2 quart casserole, cover. During last 30 minutes of roasting time bake stuffing mixture with turkey. Remove turkey to platter. Drain off fat from drippings. Let rest a few seconds. Skim fat drippings. Return drippings to pan. Add gravy and heat. Serve with turkey. Makes 10 to 12 servings.

BRAISED DUCKLING

    3 1/2 - 4 lb. duckling
    4 oz. butter
    2 onions
    2 carrots
    1/4 cup brandy or wine
    1 cup chicken stock
    1/2 lb. young sliced turnips
    * salt & pepper to taste

Brown duck on all sides in a casserole. Put in the onions and sliced carrots, browning them also. Pour in the liquor and all the stock with salt and pepper. Place in a moderate oven, 350F and baste frequently. When duck is ready, keep it warm. Strain the liquid, remove vegetables and reduce the sauce. Serve with the young turnips which have been cooked while the duck was braising. Blanch the turnips first, then saute in butter.

DUCK AND PINEAPPLE

4 lb. duck
1 tin pineapple slices
2 Tbsp. oil
2 Tbsp. soya sauce
1 Tbsp. rum
1/2 cup water
2 Tbsp. brown sugar
* pinch salt

Clean and roast the duck. Cook, remove bones and slice. Drain pineapple slices and dice. Place duck and pineapple in alternate layers in a casserole. Add the pineapple juice mixed with oil, soya sauce, rum, water, sugar and salt. Bake in moderate oven for 1 hour. Serve with rice and green salad.

CHICKEN STEW

    4 lb. chicken
    * oil
    4 onions
    2 tomatoes
    2 cloves garlic
    1/2 tsp. salt
    1 cup water
    * hard boiled eggs
    * cooked white rice

Cut up chicken and saute in oil. Add diced tomatoes, onions and garlic. Finally, add all the seasoning. Mix well and fry for 5 minutes. Empty into a pot adding more water if needed and stew until flesh is tender. When cooked, float halved, hard boiled eggs on the top and serve with rice.

GOAT/MUTTON

CURRY GOAT OR MUTTON

1 lb. meat
4 Tbsp. cooking oil
1 clove garlic
2 sprigs chive
1 slice hot pepper, if preferred
2 onions
2 cups water
* small piece ginger
1-2 Tbsp. curry powder

Cut meat into one inch strips. Finely chop onions, garlic, chives, ginger (and pepper). Heat oil in pan; add seasonings and curry powder; cook for 2 minutes. Add the meat and brown in the savoury. Heat and simmer until the meat is tender. Cooking too rapidly will toughen the meat and boil away the curry sauce. When cooked, serve with hot rice. Side dishes can also be served of chopped cucumber, chopped tomato, sliced bananas, etc. Serves 4 to 5.

MUTTON STEW

Goat Meat or Mutton

3 lbs. goat meat (mutton)
* oil, salt, flour
4 cups hot water
1 tsp. hot sauce
1 cup chopped onions
1 cup sliced carrots
1 cup chopped tomatoes
1 cup sliced potatoes
* some small flour dumplings

   Dredge cubed meat with flour and salt, and brown in hot oil. Add water and simmer until meet is tender. Add sauce, onions and vegetables. Cook until vegetables are ready. This process should take about 2 hours. When all is ready, add the dumplings which will cook very quickly. Add more liquid if necessary.

FISH

ESCOVEITCHED FISH

1 1/2 -2 lbs. snapper or king fish
1/2 cup vinegar
2 medium sized onions
1 green and 1 ripe pepper
* few pimento seeds
* salt & pepper

Have fish cleaned and cut in fillets or slices. Season with salt and pepper and fry in oil. Cut the onions in rings and slice the peppers. Bring the vinegar and pimento seeds to a boil. Lay fish slices in a shallow dish. Pour on the vinegar and leave for 1 hour, turning occasionally. Serve hot or cold.

SNAPPER IN BUTTER

8 oz. deboned snapper
4 oz. flour
1 egg
Pinch salt.
1/2 cup milk, or a tip of milk and ice water
Oil for frying

Sieve flour and salt in a bowl, beat in egg yolk and milk, fold in beaten egg white, coat fish with batter. Fry until golden brown, drain on absorbent paper. Serve hot with the following sauce.

Sauce:

1 onion,
1 oz. margarine,
1/4 cup soya sauce,
a piece of dry ginger,
1/4 cup water,
1/2 sweet pepper,
1 Tbsp. sugar,
2 Tbsp. ketchup.

Saute onion in margarine. Add remaining ingredients and allow to simmer. Thicken sauce with cornstarch.

CURRIED KING FISH

1 1/2 lb. deboned king fish
1 Tbsp. curry, salt to taste
1 small onion
1 stalk chopped escallion
1 tsp. chopped pepper
2 Tbsp. oil, 1 Tbsp. margarine, 1/2 cup water

Dice fish and saute until lightly brown and firm. Add all other ingredients and cook until done. Serve with steamed white rice or boiled green bananas.

KINGFISH IN COCONUT CREAM

2 lb. fish steaks
3 oz. butter or margarine
1/2 cup coconut cream
* salt & pepper
* lime slices

Heat butter and fry steaks until brown on both sides.

To make coconut cream, grate a coconut, add water, squeeze and strain out cream. Discard pulp.

Add to fish steaks with salt and pepper. Simmer for about 3 minutes. Garnish with lime slices.

KING FISH FILLETS

4 fillets king fish
1 glass white wine
* pinch salt & pepper
* squeeze of lime juice
1 cup cooked and peeled shrimps
1 cup white sauce
1 egg
1 cup bread crumbs
2-3 Tbsp. margarine or oil
2 Tbsp. tomato sauce

Soak fillets in white wine, salt, pepper and lime juice for 1 hour. Remove and pat dry.

Make 1 cup of white sauce and add the cooked shrimps. When this is cool, spoon some of mixture onto each fish fillet and roll up. Dip in bread crumbs, then into beaten egg and again in crumbs. Fry in hot oil. Serve with tomato sauce.

CURRIED LOBSTER AND RICE

1 medium or 2 small lobsters
2 slices green lime or lemon
Bay leaf, salt, pepper, slice onion
2 cups rice

Boil the lobster for 20 minutes with lime or lemon, bay leaf, salt, pepper and onion. Break open, preserving the back and tail shell. Cut the meat into small cubes.

Make a curry sauce from 1 cup of coconut cream, stock or cream of chicken or mushroom soup, 2 Tbsp. curry, 1/4 tsp. ginger, dash of picapepper. Heat the lobster in the sauce and pile into the shells. Serve with mango chutney and Bombay duck.

Boil the rice in 4 cups water, steaming until grains are loose and thoroughly cooked.

PEPPER SHRIMPS

1 pint shrimps
* white vinegar, water
* sliced hot pepper (remove the seeds)
1/2 sliced onion
* salt and pimento grains

Cover shrimps with salted water and boil until tender. Cool, peel and clean them. Meanwhile mix vinegar, peppers, onions and pimento grains. Bring to a boil, pour over shrimps and store in a covered jar for 12 hours before serving.

CRAB BACKS

The back crab (seasonal) is considered a delicacy. Boil 12 crabs and carefully remove all the meat. Save the backs. Mince the meat. Mix 4 Tbsp. browned bread crumbs, black pepper, 1 Tbsp. minced onion, 1/2 tsp. good curry powder. Mix all with the crab meat. Fill the backs with crab mixture, topping with bread crumbs and dots of butter. Bake for 15 to 20 minutes till brown.

SWEET & SOUR PERCH

2 lbs. perch
1 tsp. black pepper, salt to taste
lime juice
seasoned flour
oil

Clean fish and debone and cut into one inch cubes; season well. Add lime juice. Dip fish into seasoned flour and fry in heated oil until golden brown. Add sweet & sour sauce, and simmer.

SEAFOOD DELIGHT

2 onions (chopped finely)
2 cloves garlic
2 green peppers (chopped finely)
6 Tbsp. fresh parsley
1/2 cup celery, chopped
1/2 cup oil
4 Tbsp. flour
1/2 lb. hot sausage
2 fresh crabs
2 sprigs fresh thyme
1 fresh tomato
1 qt. water
1 tsp. sugar
* salt, pepper & cayenne to taste
1 lb. fresh shrimp

Saute onion, garlic, green peppers, parsley, celery in oil until lightly brown. Add flour and cook 3 minutes. Add hot sausage, crabs, thyme, tomatoes, water, sugar, salt, pepper and cayenne. Boil for 20 minutes. Add shrimp and cook for 15 minutes.

MACKEREL COO-COO

1 tin drained mackerel
1/2 cup diced pineapple
2 Tbsp. chopped peanuts
1/4 cup mayonnaise
1 Tbsp. limo juice

Break up mackerel. Combine remaining ingredients and toss. Serve in shells or lettuce cups. Sardines can also be served in this manner.

BEER BATTER FOR FISH

1/4 cup cornstarch
3/4 cup flour
1/4 cup beer
2 egg whites
* salt to taste, black pepper
1/4 cup margarine or oil
Any type of fish may be used.

Mix cornstarch, flour, pepper and salt. Add beer and beat until smooth. Beat egg whites and fold into batter. Dip slices of fish or whole small fish into this batter and fry in bubbling oil.

SALT COD AND ACKEE

(Ackee and Salt Fish)

1 lb. salt fish
12/14 ackees
2 oz. fried bacon
4 oz. margarine
2 Tbsp. chopped tomatoes
2 Tbsp. chopped onion
* pepper

Soak fish overnight and discard the water. Cover with cold water and boil until tender. Skin, bone and flake, and set aside. Prepare ackees and boil quickly. In a separate pan, melt margarine, stir in onions, tomatoes and pepper. Simmer a few minutes, then add the fish and ackees. Heat through and serve.

CODFISH LAID

1/2 lb. cod fish
1 Tbsp. butter
1 dessert spoonful lard
slice of yam
4 large potatoes
escallion, pepper
tomato, herbs

Soak and boil the fish. Wash and cook potatoes and yam. Chop fish and mix well with the cooked potatoes and yam. Add lard, herbs and other ingredients. Mix in a beaten egg. Butter a pie dish, put in the mixture an bake to a light brown.

CURRIED CODFISH

1/2 lb. salt codfish
2 Tbsp. minced onion
1 Tbsp. curry powder
1 tsp. lime juice
* flour
* salt

Wash fish and cut into strips. Flour lightly and fry in bubbling oil. Remove the fish and fry onion in the pan. Sprinkle with curry powder and moisten with lime juice. Allow to simmer, then add slices of fish and heat through. Serve with rice.

CODFISH FRITTERS

1/2 lb. cod fish
1 Tbsp butter
* chopped fresh pepper (or cayenne)
* tomatoes, escallion, parsley
2 well beaten eggs
* oil

Boil the fish and mash it fine with seasoning, butter, pepper and tomatoes, escallions and herb. Mix well with eggs and fry in hot oil.

FISH PATTIES

    1 lb. perch deboned
    1 small onion chopped
    1 hot pepper
    1 sprig thyme
    2 Tbsp. margarine
    1 cup water
    2 tsp. soya sauce
    2 slices bread, soaked and crushed

Dice perch. Saute chopped onion, hot pepper and theme in margarine. Add perch and brown lightly then add water. Continue cooking until fish is quite soft. Add soya sauce, bread and salt. Continue cooking, but do not overcook as filling should not be too dried out.

FISH PIE

2 cups cooked flaked fish
1 cup white sauce
1 cup cooked peeled shrimps
* salt, pepper, chopped parsley
1 cup cooked, mashed potatoes
1 cup flour
* pinch salt
1 beaten egg

Mix together fish, white sauce, shrimp, seasonings and parsley, and place in deep pie dish. Mix remaining ingredients to form a dough. Roll out on a floured board and cut to cover pie. Place over fish mixture and prick top with a fork. Bake in a moderate oven about 20 minutes, or till crust is brown.

DRESSINGS & SAUCES

CURRY SAUCE

1 oz. unsalted butter
1 onion, finely chopped
1 small carrot, scraped and finely chopped
1 small stalk celery, chopped
1/2 tsp. ground ginger
1 Tbsp. curry powder
1 Tbsp. plain flour
1/2 pint beef stock
* salt, freshly ground pepper
1/4 pint coconut milk, or single cream
1 tsp. lime or lemon juice

In a heavy saucepan, heat the butter and saute onion, carrot and celery until the onion is tender and lightly browned. Add the ginger, curry powder and flour and cook, stirring for 3 or 4 minutes longer. Add the flour and stock, season with salt and pepper, mix, cover and simmer gently for 30 minutes. Add the coconut milk and cook until heated through. Remove from the heat and stir in the lime juice.

DEVILS SAUCE

2 Tbsp. brown sugar
1 dessert spoon creole sauce
3 Tbsp. ketchup
1/4 tsp. hot sauce
1 Tbsp. guava jelly
1/4 tsp. salt
2 Tbsp. vinegar

Mix all ingredients together in a saucepan and simmer for 2 minutes. Cool and chill.

HOT PEPPER SAUCE

4 hot peppers
1 tsp. oil
1 tsp. creole sauce
1 tsp. ketchup
1 tsp. vinegar
* salt to taste

Put peppers and other ingredients through a blender or mincer. Bottle. Makes 1 bottle.

SPICY DRESSING

3 Tbsp. vinegar
2 Tbsp. sugar
1 Tbsp. powdered sugar

Blend together and chill. Delicious on crisp green salad.

A DRESSING FOR SEA FOOD

4 Tbsp. mayonnaise
4 Tbsp. french dressing
2 Tbsp. mango chutney
1 tsp. lime juice
* pinch of curry powder
* salt and pepper to taste

Combine and mix all ingredients.

INGREDIENTS FOR SWEET AND SOUR SAUCE

1 cup pineapple or orange juice
1 Tbsp. tomato sauce
1 small carrot sliced thinly
1 small ripe sweet pepper, cut into strips
1/2 oz. ginger, roll out into thin slivers
3 Tbsp. brown sugar
4 Tbsp. vinegar
1 Tbsp. cornstarch
1 onion sliced
1 tsp, mono sodium glutamate
3 Tbsp. dry sherry (optional)

Place all ingredients in a saucepan and simmer on appropriate meat dishes.

ROTI/PATTIES

ROTI

2 cups flour
1/4 tsp. baking soda
1/4 tsp. salt
Milk to mix

Sift flour, soda and salt together. Add enough milk to mix to a stiff dough. Form small pieces into balls & roll out flat with a rolling pin. Dot with softened butter. Fold into a ball & roll out again. Cook on a hot baking stove or iron. Test heat first by sprinkling flour on stove. If it browns at once it is hot enough. Lay roti on hot stove and turn constantly while cooking.

PELAU

1 boiling fowl
6 slices bacon
2 Tbsp. fat
2 eggs, hard boiled
2 cups rice
1 onion, chopped
1/2 cup cooked tomatoes

Boil fowl until tender; cut into joints and fry with bacon. Brown onion in fat; add cooked tomatoes, rice and 1 cup of chicken stock in which fowl was boiled. Cook until rice is soft and splitting, adding more stock as required to keep rice moist. Pile rice on a dish, lay chicken and bacon alternately round it and garnish with egg slices.

CORNMEAL DUMPLINGS

3 Tbsp. shortening
1/2 tsp. baking powder
1/2 cup flour
1/2 cup cornmeal
1/8 tsp. salt

Mix all ingredients and add enough cold water to make a stiff dough. Form into balls and lay on top of Sancoche or in soup and cook 20 minutes.

BEEF PATTIES

4 cups flour
1 Tbsp curry
1 tsp. salt
1/2 lb. shortening or lard
* iced water
2 onions
2 oz. escallion
2 hot peppers
2 lbs. minced beef
2 oz. oil
1/2 lb. bread crumbs
3 springs thyme
2 Tbsp. curry powder
1 Tbsp. salt
1 cup water

Pastry: Sift together flour, curry and salt. Work in shortening and enough water to hold dough together. Refrigerate in foil for 12 hours. Remove 15 minutes before use, pulling off just enough to make one patty at a time. Roll out and cut into 6" circles. Flour and stack. Cover with damp cloth.

Filling: Mince onions, escallion and hot peppers. Add to minced beef. Heat oil in frying pan, add minced beef and stir for 10 minutes. Add bread crumbs, thyme, curry powder and salt. Mix well then add water. Simmer for further 1/2 hour. Cool.

Fill the prepared pastry circles with filling. Fold over and seal by crimping edges with fork. Bake on ungreased baking sheets in preheated oven at 400F for 30-35 minutes until brown. Makes approx. 3 doz.

TIE-A-LEAF

1 lb. cornmeal
1/2 lb. sugar
1 tsp. mixed spice
1 tsp. salt
2 tsp. vanilla
2 oz. flour
1/2 cup grated coconut
1 tsp. cinnamon
1 Tbsp. molasses
2 1/2 cups coconut "milk" or reconstituted skimmed milk

Blend all dry ingredients and grated coconut thoroughly. Mix together "milk", molasses, vanilla and add to dry ingredients stirring briskly.

Variations: Place 1/2 cup to 1 cup of mixture into quailed banana bark or pour 1 cup of the mixture into cooking bags and tie the bag with twine. Put the small parcels into boiling water, enough to cover and cook for 40 minutes or until done. Serves 4 to 6.

VEGETABLES

RICE AND PEAS

1 cup red peas (soaked overnight)
2 qts. hot water
1 slice salt pork or beef
3 cups rice
1 sliced onion
1 sprig thyme
* piece of hot pepper
1 grated coconut or 2 oz. coconut cream
1 Tbsp. oil
* salt

Brown onion with salt pork and seasoning. Meanwhile, add 1 cup hot water to grated coconut and squeeze out cream. Place peas in a pot with coconut cream. Add seasonings and water and cook with rice over medium heat until peas are tender (adding more water if necessary) and until liquid is absorbed and rice is cooked.

SEASONED RICE

1/2 lb. rice
1/4 lb. salt beef
1/4 lb. pigs tail
1 medium carrot
1 small eggplant
I Tbsp. margarine
1 small onion
3 leaves cabbage
1 medium sized tomato
1 tsp. black pepper; 1 tsp. salt.
* Chives or thyme

Clean and wash meat. Cook in cold water for 45 minutes (until partially tender). Wash and dice carrot and eggplant. Cut onion, tomato and cabbage finely. Wash chives and thyme and tie in a bundle. Add carrot to meat and cook about 10 minutes. Add greens and eggplant and cook for 5 minutes. Add rice, seasoning and margarine. Cook about 25 minutes until rice is tender. Serve hot.

BAKED SWEET POTATO

Allow 1/2 potato per person
3 baked potatoes in skin
2 Tbsp. grated coconut
3 Tbsp. Red Stripe Beer
2 oz. butter
* salt, cinnamon

Cut potatoes in half, scoop out pulp. Crush with beer and butter. Add coconut and salt. Sprinkle with cinnamon and bake through to heat and serve.

SEASONED OR TURNED CORNMEAL

    4 oz. corned pork
    3 cups warm water
    1 small tomato, chopped
    1/4 tsp. chopped pepper
    1 oz, margarine or butter
    1 dry coconut
    1 stalk escallion or 1 small onion, chopped
    2 cups cornmeal

Rinse pork and fry in a heavy duty pot. Grate coconut; save 1/2 cup and extract "milk" from the rest with three cups warm water. Bring 2 cups "milk" to the boil, add fried meat seasonings. Moisten cornmeal and grated coconut with 1 cup coconut milk and add with butter or margarine to pot, stirring briskly. Lower flame and simmer for 10 to 15 minutes. Serve hot or pack into greased loaf pan for mold. Unmold when slightly cool, slice and serve cold or fry lightly on both sides.

N.B. Cod fish, deboned and flaked or chopped left over meats may be substituted for pork.

COO COO

From the Eastern Caribbean

4-6 medium Okras
1 tsp. salt
1 cup cornmeal
2 cups water
1/4 lb. cooked salted meat or fish
1 Tbsp. butter or margarine

Cook sliced okra in 1 cup boiling water to which salt has been added. Add diced cooked meat or fish. Mix the cornmeal with 1 cup cold water and stir into pot. Add margarine or butter. Cook until thick and smooth stirring vigorously to get the okras well blended. Turn into greased basin or pan. Unmold. Serve with fish. Serves 2 to 3.

POTATO OMELET

3 eggs, separated
1 cup mashed potatoes
1/4 tsp. onion juice
1/2 tsp. minced parsley
1 tsp. salt
1/4 tsp. pepper
3 Tbsp. cream or milk

Add egg yolks to potatoes and heat until there are no lumps. Add onion juice, parsley, salt, pepper and cream or milk. Beat egg whites until stiff and fold into potato mixture. Transfer to greased frying pan and bake in moderately slow over (325F) until brown. Then turn and fold on hot platter.

DESSERTS

BANANA DELIGHT

3 ripe bananas
1/2 cup rum
1 Tbsp. sugar
1 tsp. lime juice
8 oz. flour
1/2 oz. butter
9 Tbsp. milk
1 tsp. baking powder
1 egg
* oil

Peel bananas and cut into thick chunks. Soak banana chunks into the delight using a perforated spoon. Fry lightly in hot oil.

RIPE BANANA PIE

2 slices bananas
1 pkg. lime jello - prepared as per instructions
* cherries
* shredded coconut (optional)

Place sliced bananas in a pre-baked pie shell. Cover with cooked lime jello mixture. Chill. Decorate with cherries and shredded coconut.

BANANA PUDDING

6 ripe crushed bananas
3 Tbsp. melted butter
1 glass white wine
1/2 lb. sugar
3 beaten egg whites
* vanilla to taste

Mix all together and heat until smooth. Put into a souffle dish and bake at 325F until puffy and golden brown on top. Serve at once. The yolk may be used to make sauce to serve with the pudding.

COCONUT CREAM PIE

1 1/2 cups milk
1/4 cup grated coconut
3 eggs, separated
4 Tbsp. sugar
1 tsp. vanilla and a pinch of salt
2 cups flour
1 cup margarine
4 Tbsp. ice water - salt to taste

Heat milk and set aside, beat yolks and add sugar, vanilla, salt and coconut. Stir in heated milk and fold in stiffly beaten egg whites.

Mix together flour, margarine, water and salt to form a dough. Roll out and line a pie dish. Prick the bottom. Pour in filling and bake for 50 minutes in a 350F oven.

BROWN SUGAR PIE

    2 cups brown sugar
    4 eggs
    2 Tbsp. vanilla
    1 partially baked 9" shell
    11/2 tsp. cornstarch
    3 Tbsp. evaporated milk
    1 tsp. lime juice

Preheat oven to 325F. Combine sugar and beat in eggs once at a time. Stir in evaporated milk, lime juice and vanilla. Blend in melted margarine or butter. Pour into shell. Bake until brown and puffed. Cool and serve.

PEANUT PIE

3 to 4 cups peanut butter
1 cup sugar (white)
3 eggs
1 to 3 cups milk
1 partially baked 9" pie shell
1/2 cup butter or margarine
1 cup brown sugar
2 Tbsp. flour
1 tsp. vanilla

Preheat oven to 325F. Melt peanut butter and butter in a saucepan. Remove from heat. Combine sugar, eggs, flour, milk and vanilla. Blend in peanut mixture. Pour into pie shell. Bake for about 1 hour. Cool to serve.

LIME PIE

2 egg yolks
4 oz. condensed milk
1/4 cup lime juice
1 egg white
* salt
6 Tbsp. sugar
3 egg whites
1 baked pie shell

Beat yolks, stir in milk and add lime juice gradually. Beat well. Whip egg whites with a pinch of salt and fold into mixture. Pour into a baked pie shell and cover with meringue. Bake until meringue is golden brown.

ORANGE DESSERT

2 cups milk
2 Tbsp. cornstarch
1 cup sugar
4 egg yolks
1 Tbsp. cold water
3/4 cup orange juice
1 tsp. orange rind
1 pint whipped cream
* sponge cake slices

Heat milk in double boiler. Mix cornstarch, sugar and yolks and pour into warm milk. Cook slowly for 10 minutes. Dissolve gelatin into warm water and add juice and rind. Place in refrigerator to chill and thicken. Line a spring form pan with slices of sponge cake. Pour mixture over this and chill. Just before serving, top with some whipped cream.

CAKES & BREADS

BANANA BREAD

1 cup sugar
1/4 cup margarine or butter
3 crushed, ripe bananas
2 cups flour
1 unbeaten egg
1 tsp. baking powder
1/2 tsp. soda
* vanilla flavouring

Cream sugar and butter. Add bananas and mix well. Add egg and dry ingredients and vanilla. Beat well. Bake in a greased, paper lined loaf tin at 350F for 50 minutes. This freezes well.

WHOLE WHEAT BREAD

2 loaves

2 cups milk or 1 cup milk and 1/4 cup honey
1 cup water
1 Tbsp. salt
1/4 cup shortening
1 cake compress or yeast
5 1/2 cups whole wheat flour, freshly ground

Scald milk and cool to luke warm; add salt and shortening. Put honey and yeast in mixing bowl, let stand until yeast is softened. Add milk and 2 cups of flour. Beat thoroughly. Add another cup of flour and beat again. Add remainder of flour. Turn out on floured board and knead until no longer sticky; this requires about 8 minutes. Place in slightly greased bowl and let rise again. Shape into two loaves and place in greased pans. Let rise until double in bulk. Bake at 375F for about 50 minutes or until nicely browned and loaf begins to shrink from the pan. Keep at even temperature (85F) for rising.

ORANGE BREAD

1 cup minced orange peel
1 cup orange juice
2 1/2 cups sugar
1 beaten egg
3 1/2 cups flour
1 cup milk
1/2 tsp. melted butter
2 tsp. baking powder
* pinch of salt

Combine orange peel and juice, and boil until peel is tender. Add 1 1/2 cups sugar, and boil slowly until thick and syrupy. Cool. Mix egg, 1 cup sugar, butter and milk. Sift flour with baking powder and salt. Add mixture and stir. Add orange mixture to dough and blend well. Pour into 2 loaf tins which have been greased and floured. Bake at 350F for 40 minutes. This is good toasted with cheese spread.

GINGER BREAD

2 cups sifted flour
2 tsp. baking powder
1 tsp. salt
1/2 tsp. ginger
1/2 tsp. cloves
3/4 cup milk
1/2 tsp. nutmeg
1/2 cup shortening
1/3 cup sugar
1/2 cup honey
2 eggs

Combine first seven ingredients and sift together three times. Cream shortening. Add sugar and honey and beat well. Add 1/2 cup of sifted dry ingredients and mix thoroughly. Add beaten eggs. Add remainder of dry ingredients alternately with milk. Bake in greased pan (375F) about 35 to 40 minutes. Cut into squares and top with honey marinque.

HONEY GINGER CAKE

2 1/2 cups sifted cake flour
1/4 tsp. baking soda
1 tsp. baking powder
1 tsp. cinnamon
1 tsp. salt
1 tsp. ground ginger
1 cup sour milk
1/2 cup butter
1/2 cup brown sugar
1 egg unbeaten
1 cup honey

Sift flour. Add baking soda, baking powder, cinnamon, salt and ginger, and sift together 3 times. Cream butter thoroughly, add sugar gradually and cream together until light and fluffy. Add egg and beat thoroughly. Add flour alternately with sour milk, a small amount at a time, beating after each addition until smooth. Bake in two well greased 9" layer pans in moderate oven (350F) for 30 minutes.

COCONUT LAYER CAKE

2/3 cups soft shortening
1 1/2 cups sugar
3 eggs
2 1/4 cups flour
2 1/2 tsp. baking powder
1 tsp. salt
1 cup milk
1 1/2 tsp. vanilla

Cream shortening & sugar until luffy. Beat in eggs, shift dry ingredients and mix in alternately with the milk. Mix thoroughly, adding the vanilla last. Pour into prepared pans and bake until done. Cool and finish with coconut filling and frosting.

RUM CAKE

1/2 cup butter
1 cup sugar
3 beaten eggs
3 cups flour
1/4 tsp. salt
1/2 tsp. baking powder
* mixed spices
1/4 cup milk
* pinch of baking soda
1/4 cup molasses
2 cups peanuts (crushed)
1 lb. raisins
1/2 cup rum

Cream butter, sugar and eggs. Mix flour, baking powder, salt and spices. Add this to butter mixture and blend. Add mil, soda and molasses and add lastly crushed nuts, raisins and rum. Bake in a loaf tin, 300F oven for 2 hours.

PEANUT BREAD

1/2 cupful blanched and chopped nuts
1/2 cup milk
1 egg beaten
2 cups sifted flour
1/2 cup sugar
2 tsp. baking powder

Mix these ingredients, make into small loaves or biscuits. Leave for one half hour. Bake in a slow oven until done, which will require about 50 minutes.

GINGERBREAD CAKE

1/2 cup shortening
1 egg
1 1/2 cups sifted all purpose flour
3/4 tsp. soda
1/2 tsp. ground cinnamon
1/2 cup sugar
1/2 cup light molasses
3/4 tsp. salt
1/2 tsp. ground ginger
1/2 cup boiling water

Preheat oven to 350F. Grease and lightly flour an 8"x8"x2" baking pan. Mix together the shortening and sugar in a large bowl until it looks creamy. Add the egg and molasses, then beat the mixture thoroughly. Stir the dry ingredients together in a small bowl. Add the dry mixture to the creamed mixture, alternately with the boiling water. Make sure you beat the mixture after each ingredient addition. Pour into baking pan and bake until done. (Insert a clean toothpick in the centre of the gingerbread. If it comes out clean, the cake is done)

BULLA CAKES

3 cups flour
8 oz. brown sugar
2 Tbsp. melted butter
2 oz. water
1 tsp. baking powder
1/2 tsp. soda
1 tsp. nutmeg
1/2 tsp. ginger powder

Make a syrup of water and sugar. Sift together dry ingredients and add syrup and melted butter. Turn onto a floured board and pat into 1/4" thickness. Cut into circles. Place on a greased tin and bake for 20 minutes in a 400F oven.

BANANA PUDDING

6 grated green bananas
2 Tbsp. flour
1 cup coconut milk
2 Tbsp. shredded coconut
2 eggs
2 Tbsp. raisins
1 oz. margarine
1 cup brown sugar
1/2 tsp. nutmeg
1/4 tsp. salt
1/2 tsp. vanilla

Add 1/2 cup milk to banana. Beat until there are no lumps. Add all other ingredients and beat again. Pour into greased dish. Bake 40 minutes. Decorate when cooled with grated coconut.

POTATO PONE

Pudding

6 lbs. grated, pared raw sweet potatoes
3/4 cup melted butter or margarine
2 tsp. grated nutmeg
2 tsp. cinnamon
1 ground ginger
2 tsp. salt
3 cups brown sugar
1 cup flour
4 cups coconut milk

Mix all together thoroughly and bake in a buttered baking dish in 350F oven about 1 1/2 hours or until well baked.

COCONUT LOAF CAKE

1/2 cup butter
1 1/2 cups sugar
2 2/3 cups flour
3/4 cup milk
2 eggs
4 tsp. baking powder
1 cup grated coconut
1 tsp. vanilla

Cream butter and 1/2 of the sugar. Beat eggs with rest of sugar and combined the mixtures. Mix in flour and baking powder, adding milk alternately with the dry ingredients. Add coconut and vanilla. Bake 1 hour in a 350F oven.

ORANGE CAKE

3 oranges
2 eggs
3/4 cup sugar
2 cups flour
1/2 cup soda and a tip of salt
1 cup butter
1/4 cup grated orange rind

Squeeze juice from oranges to make 1 cup and reserve. Cream butter and sugar and add eggs one at a time beating continuously. Add flour, salt and soda sifted together. Add 1/4 cup of orange rind and juice. Pour into greased 13" x 9" pan and bake in a moderate oven until firm.

HONEY BISCUITS

2 cups flour
1/2 tsp. salt
1 tsp. sugar
4 tsp. baking powder
1/2 cup shortening
3/4 cup milk
3 Tbsp. honey butter

Sift together flour, salt, sugar and baking powder. With form, work shortening into flour until consistency of corn meal. Add milk. Knead gently on flour board. Roll out to 1/2" each. Place on baking sheet. Combine honey and butter. Place 1/2 tsp. of mixture on each indentation. Set aside for 10 minutes. Bake at 425F for 10 to 12 minutes

PEANUT ROLLS

2 cups soft white bread crumbs
4 Tbsp. peanut butter
1 cupful grated coconut, chopped fine
1 tsp. salt
1 egg, well beaten
1/2 lb. blanched and ground peanuts

Mix together. Make into rolls and fry in a deep fat or bake in an oven. Serve with nut sauce.

SWEET POTATO COOKIES

1 1/2 cups flour
2 Tbsp. brown sugar
4 tsp. butter
* cinnamon
1 cup crushed boiled, sweet potato
1/2 cup milk

Combine all but milk and potatoes and mix until crumbly. Stir in crushed potatoes and milk. Spoon batter onto a sheet. Bake in a quick oven. Split and serve with honey and butter. Makes approximately one dozen.

EVERYDAY COOKIES

1/2 cup shortening
1/2 cup sugar
1/2 cup honey
1 egg
2/3 cup flour
1/2 tsp. baking powder
1/2 tsp. soda
1/4 tsp. salt
1 cup quick cooking oats
1 cup shredded coconut
1 tsp vanilla
1/2 cup chopped nuts

Cream shortening, sugar and honey together until light and fluffy. Add well beaten egg, blend together. Sift flour with dry ingredients, stir well. Add oats, coconut and vanilla, add nuts. Spread on greased baking sheet. Bake in moderate oven (350F). Bake about 15 to 30 minutes. Cut into bars.

COCONUT COOKIES

3/4 cup sugar
1/4 lb. butter
1 1/2 cups flour
1 tsp. baking powder
1 1/2 cups grated coconut
1 egg, beaten

Cream butter and sugar. Add flour and baking powder. Mix well then add grated coconut and egg. Mix to a paste. Drop onto a greased cookie sheet by teaspoonful. Bake at 350F for 15 minutes. Makes approx. 2 dozen.

PEANUT BUTTER COOKIES

1/2 cup brown sugar
1/2 cup white sugar
1/2 cup peanut butter
3/4 cup fat
1 egg
2 cups flour
1 tsp. soda
1/8 tsp. salt
1/2 tsp. baking powder

Cream the brown sugar and fat. Add the peanut butter and mix well. Beat the eggs and add to the butter and sugar. Mix well and chill. Make into small balls. Place on a cookie sheet 2 inches apart. Flatten with a fork, Bake in a moderate oven (350F) for 12 to 15 minutes.

PEANUT BRITTLE

2 cups granulated sugar
1 tsp. salt
1 pint peanuts, finely chopped

Put the sugar into an iron frying pan and heat slowly, stirring constantly, until the sugar is melted and turns a light brown. Have in readiness the finely chopped peanuts sprinkled with salt. Place these in a buttered tin, warm slightly and pour the melted sugar over them.

SWEET POTATO FRITTERS

1 egg
3/4 cup mashed boiled sweet potatoes
1/2 cup milk
1 1/4 cup all purpose flour
1/4 tsp. baking soda
1 1/3 tsp. baking powder
Sugar
1/2 tsp. grated nutmeg
1/2 tsp. cinnamon powder
1 1/2 tsp. rosewater and almond
* pinch salt
1/4 cup cooking oil

Beat egg until white and yolk are blended together. Combine mashed sweet potatoes with egg. Pour in milk and combine well together. Sift together flour, baking soda and baking powder. Sprinkle on sugar, nutmeg and cinnamon. Pour on rose water and almond. Heat oil in a Dutch pot or other frying utensil. For each fritter, drop one dessert spoonful of batter into oil. Fry fritters on both sides until dark brown - not burnt. Drain on absorbent paper. Lightly sprinkle sugar on top of each fritter.

PUMPKIN FRITTERS

Half a small pumpkin
1 egg
Butter
Lard
Pepper

Boil a small pumpkin until tender and then mash well with a little black pepper and one egg. When well mixed, put it in spoonfuls in a larded saucepan and fry, turning on each side until cooked. Omitting the pepper and substituting sugar to taste.

BANANA CHIPS

Select 3 fingers green bananas
1 tsp. salt
1 pint water
Fat to fry

Wash and peel bananas. Cut into strips (approx. 3" x 1/4"), soak in salt water for 5 minutes. Dry well. Fry in hot fat until golden brown.

COCONUT GIZZADAS

1 lb. brown sugar
1/4 pint water
1 grated coconut
1/2 tsp. nutmeg
2 cups flour
1/4 tsp. salt
1/4 cup margarine
* iced water to blend

Filling: Make a syrup of sugar and water. Add coconut and nutmeg. Mix well. Cool and fill pastry shells.

Pastry shells: Mix flour and salt, cut in margarine and water. Roll out and cut into circles.

Mould into cases and pinch up edges. Fill with mixture and bake in 400F oven until pastry shells are golden brown.

CORNMEAL MUFFINS

1 cup cornmeal
2/3 cup flour
1/4 tsp. soda
2 Tbsp. sugar
2 tsp. baking powder
1/2 tsp. salt
1 egg (well beaten)
3 Tbsp. melted shortening
1 cup sour milk

Grease muffin pans with 12 3" cups and set aside. Combine dry ingredients in a bowl. Add beaten egg and melted shortening to sour milk. Stir lightly with a fork until ingredients are just blended and spoon into muffin cups to make about 1/4 full. No baking powder is used then dumplings are to be boiled.

WHOLE WHEAT BANANA MUFFINS

1 cup uncooked oats
1 cup whole wheat flour
3 Tbsp. granulated sugar
2 1/2 tsp. baking powder
1/2 tsp. salt
1 large egg
1 cup mashed ripe banana
2 Tbsp. vegetable oil
1/4 cup milk

Heat oven to 400F. Grease twelve 2-1/2" muffin cups or line with paper baking cups. Mix oats, flour, sugar, baking powder and salt in a large bowl. Beat egg in medium-sized bowl, stir in banana, milk and oil; add to oat mixture, stirring just until combined. Spoon about 3 Tbsp. batter into each prepared muffin cup. Bake 15 to 20 minutes, or until a cake tester inserted in centre comes out clean. Put pan on a wire rack to cool. Makes 12.

BANANA MUFFINS

6 1/2 oz. flour
1 Tbsp. cornflour
1 tsp. baking powder
1/2 tsp. soda and a pinch of salt
2 oz. butter
3 oz. sugar
1 egg
3 crushed bananas

Sift together, flour, cornflour, baking powder, soda and salt. Cream butter and sugar. Beat egg and mix into creamed mixture. Add dry ingredients and crushed bananas alternately. Do not beat, but mix well. Bake in greased muffin containers in 400F oven for 20 minutes.

CHRISTMAS PUDDING

1 lb. raisins
1/2 lb. prunes
1/4 lb. cherries
1/4 lb. mixed peel
2 cups rum
6 cups port
1/2 tsp. grated nutmeg
1/2 tsp. ground cinnamon
2 oz. dark sugar
1/4 cup flour
1 cup bread crumbs
1 tsp baking powder
1/2 tsp. salt
1/2 lb. butter
1/2 lb. dark sugar
6 eggs
1/4 lb. chopped nuts
rind of lime
1 Tbsp. vanilla

Mince raisins, prunes, cherries, mixed peel. Add rum, 4 cups port and spices. Allow to soak for at least 2 weeks.

Simmer soaked fruit with 2 cups port stirring constantly for 15 minutes. Leave to cool.

Make dark colouring from dark sugar over low heat until liquid and very dark.

Sift together flour, bread crumbs, baking powder and salt. Cream butter, adding gradually sugar, then eggs individually, mixing well. Add cold fruit, dark colouring, then dry ingredients. Add nuts, rind of lime and vanilla.

Pour into lined 9" baking tin to 1" from top. Place greased paper on top of pudding and secure with cover. Place a pie tin upside down in a large pot. Place pudding on top and add water to 1/2 depth of pudding. Bring to a boil, lower heat to medium and maintain water level to 1/2 depth until pudding leaves sides of baking tin - approx. 3 hours. Serve cold with "hard" sauce.

CEREALS

CORNMEAL PORRIDGE

2 oz. cornmeal
1/4 tsp. salt
1/2 cup skimmed milk powder
1 pint water
4 Tbsp. sugar
1 tsp. vanilla

Mix cornmeal with a little of the water. Bring remainder of water to boil and stir in cornmeal and salt. Continue cooking for about 7 to 10 minutes. Mix skimmed milk powder with an additional 1/2 cup water and add to porridge. Sweeten to taste and add vanilla. Serves 3 to 4.

1. ½ cup grated coconut may be added if desired.
1. A "thick" porridge such as this offers good nourishment to any eater, but particularly the young child. Feed it to the child from a cup with a spoon.

CORN PORRIDGE

Grate a few nearly dry cobs and pass through a fairly fine sieve. Add a little salt. Gently stir 6 tablespoons into sufficient cold water to make it thick enough to pour. Pour the mixture into 5 pints of boiling water in which a few cinnamon leaves have been put. Stir constantly over a slow heat and keep simmering until cooked (about 20 minutes). Now stir in half a pint of coconut cream and half a pint of cow's milk and cook gently for another 10 minutes. Sweeten to taste with brown sugar or condensed milk.

PLANTAIN OR (BANANA) PORRIDGE

Use fresh, full fruit. Grate and stir into slightly salted water one medium sized plantain or two large bananas to a pint of water. Cook in a double boiler, stirring occasionally, or in an ordinary saucepan, stirring frequently if too thin, stir in while cooking a little sifted flour mixed with milk. When cooked, add sufficient sugar and milk, and simmer gently for 5 minutes longer. Finish with grated nutmeg.

DRINKS

PINA COLADA PUNCH

4 oz. golden rum
pineapple stick
2 oz. coconut cream
1/2 cup crushed ice
Maraschino cherry

Place all the ingredients, except the pineapple stock and cherry in an electric blender for a few seconds. Pour, unstrained into a tumbler and decorate with the pineapple stick and cherry. Serves 1.

PLANTER'S PUNCH

1 1/2 oz. dark rum
1/4 oz. lime juice
3 oz. orange juice
1/2 cup crushed ice
Maraschino cherry

Combine all the ingredients in a cocktail shaker and shake vigorously. Strain into a tumbler and garnish with the cherry. Serves 1.

PEACH DAIQUIRI

2 oz. light rum
1/2 medium-sized ripe fresh peach, peeled and coarsely chopped
1 Tbsp. caster sugar
1 cup finely crushed ice

Combine all the ingredients in an electric blender and blend at high speed for about 30 seconds. Pour into a thoroughly chilled glass and serve with short drinking straws. Serves 1.

MANGO DAIQUIRI

4 oz. light rum
1 oz. wine
1/2 cup finely chopped fresh mango
2 Tbsp. lime juice
1 Tbsp. caster sugar
2 cups finely crushed ice

Place all ingredients in an electric blender and blend at high speed until the contents have the consistency of snow. Pour into 2 thoroughly chilled champagne glasses and serve with short drinking straws. Serves 2.

PINEAPPLE DAIQUIRI

2oz. light rum
1/2 oz. Cointreau
1/4 pint pineapple juice
1 Tbsp. lime juice
Caster sugar
ice cubes

Combine the rum, Cointreau, pineapple and lime juice in an electric blender and blend quickly at high speed. Taste and blend in a little caster sugar, if necessary. Fill a glass with ice cubes and pour in the daiquiri. Serves 1.

PEANUT PUNCH

2 Tbsp. cornflour
1/2 pint water
3/4 pint milk
6 Tbsp. peanut butter
sugar to taste

Mix the cornflour and water in a small saucepan. Add the milk, peanut butter and sugar to taste. Cook, stirring with a whisk, over moderate heat until thickened and thoroughly mixed. Cool and refrigerate. Serve in tumblers, with or without ice. Serves 2.

Though this is traditionally served as a soft drink, many Trinidadians find it improved, as indeed I do, by the addition of a good Trinidadian or similar rum. Add 4 oz. rum to the above recipe and serve in tumblers with ice cubes.

MILK PUNCH

    1 egg yolk
    3/4 cup scaled milk
    * a little rum or brandy, nutmeg

Beat egg yolk and sugar together. Add scalded milk gradually, stirring constantly. Add rum and nutmeg. Serve at once.

MANGO FOO

6 bombay mangoes (ripe)
6 tsp. condensed milk
1 cup light cream
1 tsp. lime juice
* nutmeg

Peel mangoes, slice flesh off seeds and put through a blender. Add milk, cream, lime juice and nutmeg, Stir well and chill.

RUM PUNCH

1/2 lb. sugar
1 pint orange juice
1 pint lemon juice
1 pt sugar syrup
2 qts. rum
3 qts. carbonated water
1/2 pineapple, thinly sliced
2 oranges, quartered
1 lemon, thinly sliced

Serve well with ice from a punch bowl. Strain and serve into small high ball glasses if desired. Serves 12.

BRANDY MILK PUNCH

3 jiggers cognac
2 dashes rum
2 Tbsp. sugar syrup
1 Tbsp. curacao
1 cup milk
4 ice cubes

Blend 10 seconds, strain, serve in highball glasses and grate nutmeat on top.

SORREL

Roselle

Sorrel is an unusual plant, growing to about 6 feet high. At the time when the petals of the flower wither, the sepals grow bigger, becoming quite fleshy and bright red, enveloping the seed pod. It is the red sepals that are used as fruit.

Sorrel Drink #1:

Wash sorrel and take off the red sepals. Make a light syrup with 2 cups sugar and 2 cups water. Pour while boiling hot over the sorrel and leave over night. In the morning strain and bottle. Serve with ice and soda water.

Sorrel Drink #2:

3 cups sorrel sepals
Small piece of ginger
piece of dried orange peel
6 cups boiling water
2 cups sugar

Wash the sorrel and place in a jar with the ginger, orange peel and cloves. Pour on boiling water and allow to stand for 24 hours. Strain and sweeten, and pour into bottles. Use as required with ice and soda water.

SPICED FRUIT DRINK

1/2 cup water
2 Tbsp. sugar
1/2 tsp. grated orange peel
2 whole cloves
1 stick cinnamon

Combine in a saucepan and bring to boiling for 10 minutes. Strain and cool.

Pour over spice mixture

1 1/2 cups pineapple juice
1/2 cup orange juice
2 Tbsp. lime juice

Mix thoroughly. Chill and serve. Serves 3.

BULL SHOT

4 oz. chilled beef bouillon
1 jigger vodka
1/2 lime
dash tabasco
2 or 3 ice cubes

Pour bouillon and vodka into a shaker. Squeeze juice from lime half into shaker; add tabasco and ice cubes. Shake well and stain into glass. Garnish with cucumber slice.

SHERRY FLIP OVER

2 oz. sherry
1 egg
1 Tbsp. confectioners' sugar

Shake well with ice and strain into a 3-4 oz. glass. This drink may also be made with 3 oz. cream added.

PRESERVES

VEGETABLE RELISH

6 carrots
1 pepper, seed removed
2 onions
2 chochos
1 cucumber
6 olives
2 cups water

Dressing:

1/2 cup oil
1 cup vinegar
2 Tbsp. ketchup
1 Tbsp. hot pepper juice
* salt to taste

Chop carrot, pepper, onions, chochos, cucumber and olives, add water to cover. Bring to a boil to tenderize. Drain.

For dressing: Mix dressing and bring to a boil, Pour dressing over the vegetables, which have been packed in sterilized jars. Makes 4 jars.

HINTS TO PRESERVE FRESH TOMATOES

Choose firm, ripe, small tomatoes without blemishes. Put them into a jar with a large mouth. Fill jar with oil (corn oil preferably), so that tomatoes are covered with a layer of oil 1" deep. One top of oil pour a little brandy or rum and seal.

PRESERVED FRUIT IN RUM CANDID GRAPEFRUIT PEEL

Candid citrus fruit are exceptionally popular with everyone, and here is a special way to prepare grapefruit peel.

Though most often made during the Christmas season, this confection is refreshing at all times of the year and keeps well in tightly covered jars.

1 Tbsp. light rum
Water
1/2 cup honey
additional granulated sugar
peel from two large ripe grapefruits
1/2 tsp salt
1/2 cup granulated sugar

Cover crubble peel with water and add the salt. Simmer in a large sauce pan for 30 minutes. Drain, then cover with water and simmer until just tender. Drain again. Carefully remove all white inner part from peel and cut the remaining yellow peel into neat strips about 1 1/2" long and 1/4" wide, or a little longer, if desired. Bring the sugar, honey and 1/4 cup water to the boil in a heavy saucepan.

Add the grapefruit peel and simmer until desired. Stir in rum and allow peel to steep while cooling overnight. Reheat peel and syrup next day, then drain roll in the ret of the granulated sugar, and arrange on waxed paper to dry. Store in neat layers in tight covered jars.

HERB VINEGARS

Various herb vinegars can be made by loosely packing a jar with a combination of herbs and filling with vinegar. Stand jar in a saucepan of water and bring to a boil slowly. Then allow to cool. After 2 weeks vinegar will be ready to use.

PEPPER WINE

Fill 1/4 bottle with either cherry or bird peppers. Fill up with sherry or rum. Allow to stand for about 2 weeks before use.

CHOCHO JAM

\6 chocho, peeled and cut into chunks
6 bananas, peeled and sliced
4 oranges, peeled and cut into chunks
sugar
4 lemons, seeded and very thinly sliced
5 qts. water

Put all the fruit into a pan with the water and simmer for 2 hours. Measure the fruit and add 1 1/2 cups sugar for each 2 1/2 cups fruit. Warm the sugar in 325F over for a few minutes. Add the hot sugar to the fruit, stir well and boil hard to the jelling point. Stir the mixture well and out in jars. Makes about 2 pints.

PINEAPPLE JAM

1 pineapple
Sugar
Nutmeg

Peel and grate the pineapple. To each pound of pineapple pulp, add 3/4 lb. sugar. Add nutmeg to taste. Boil and stir until mixture thickens and sugar is melted. Seal in jars whilst hot. Makes approx. 3 jars.

SIMPLE CARROT JAM

6 lbs. sugar
9 cups sugar
grate and thinly sliced carrots

Place the carrots and sugar in an enamel tinned or stainless steel pan. Cook over medium heat, stirring frequently. Occasionally mash the pieces of carrots that have not yet broken up. When the jam is thick and sticky, after approx. 1 hour, put it in jars. Process according to directions in a general preserving guide. Makes about5 pints.

PUMPKIN JAM

3 lbs. pumpkin
1 lime
pinch of salt
2 lbs. sugar
1 orange

Peel and cut pumpkin into slices, then dice and pack in a jar. Add sugar. Cover and stand for 12 hours. Drain off liquid and boil until syrupy. Add pumpkin, sliced lime and orange. Stir in salt. Boil up and cook until clear. Seal in jars. Makes approx. 6 jars.

TOMATO JAM

8 tomatoes, peeled and chopped
1 cup sugar
1/2 tsp. allspice
2 Tbsp. lime juice
2 Tbsp. chopped raisins

Simmer tomatoes for 10 minutes. Add all ingredients except sugar and bring to a boil. Add sugar and continue to boil until sugar melts and mixture thickens. Skim and cool.

TOMATO MARMALADE

1 1/2 lb. large ripe tomatoes, peeled, halved and seeded
2 1/2 cups sugar
1 cup water
6 Tbsp. fresh lemon juice

Boil the sugar and water together for about 5 minutes to make a thick syrup. Stir in the tomatoes and the lemon juice. Stirring frequently, cook over medium heat for about 45 minutes, or until the tomatoes are translucent and the syrup thick. Put in jars and cover. Makes about 2 pints.

GUAVA JELLY AND ORANGE JELLY

7 lbs. guavas (do not crush fruit)
7 pints water (boil 30 minutes)
7 cups diced orange
sugar

These are made to the same formula as grape jelly (see above). Strain and measure juice in each instance, and add equal amount of sugar. Boil until liquid jells. Pour into jars. Makes approx. 4 to 5 jars.

GRAPE JELLY

7 lbs. grapes
7 pints water
sugar

Add grapes to water and bring to a boil. Stir with a wooden spoon and crush fruit while stirring. Measure this juice and for every cup of liquid add an equal amount of sugar. Return sugar and liquid to heat and boil rapidly. Skim. Boil until a little tested on a plate will jell. Pour into jars and cool before sealing. Makes approx. 4 to 5 jars.

SOFT CUSTARD

2-4 eggs
1 pint milk
3-4 Tbsp. sugar
1/2 tsp. vanilla
1/8 tsp. salt

Heat the milk, sugar and salt in a double boiler. Beat the eggs lightly and mix some of the hot milk. Pour back into the double boiler and stir constantly until the custard coats the spoon. Remove at once from the heat and set in a bowl of cold water. Add the vanilla.

TOFFEE

Toffee is a hard, brittle sweet made from sugar, butter, water and flavouring.

Use a large, strong pan and once the mixture has come to the boil, use only a gentle heat as toffee is inclined to boil over. The toffee can be stirred while the sugar is melting and coming to the boil, but not afterwards. If milk or cream is used, then a gentle stirring is allowed.

Toffee should be cooked at a temperature of 260F until it is brittle when tested in cold water (hard ball stage). When the required temperature is reached, pour the toffee quickly into a shallow, buttered pan. Do not use a spoon. Allow the toffee to cool and when lukewarm, mark into squares with a buttered knife. If the toffee is marked when too hot it will lose its shape; if too cold, it is impossible to cut.

Flavourings and colourings can be added to pulled toffee before the edges are turned to the centre before pulling.

It is essential to work quickly when pulling toffee.

PLAIN TOFFEE

1 lb. brown sugar (No.2)
1/4 cup water
3 oz. butter

Put all ingredients into a saucepan and dissolve the sugar slowly. Lower the heat as soon as the mixture comes to the boil and cook until it is brittle when tested in cold water (280F). Pour into a buttered pan to cool. This toffee can be pulled if wished.

PEANUT SCRUNCH

Make the above recipe for toffee. Have ready 1/4 cup of chopped peanuts to sprinkle over the top immediately the toffee has been poured into the pan.

GLOSSARY OF COOKING TERMS

Baine-Marie	A french cooking utensil similar to a double boiler used to cook over boiling water.
Bake	To cook by dry heat, usually in an oven.
Barbeque	Generally refers to foods cooked outdoors over an open fire with a spicy sauce.
Baste	To brush or spoon liquid over food while cooking, to keep it moist.
Batter	Any combination which incudes flour, milk, butter, eggs or the like for pancakes, coating, dipping, etc.
Beat	To mix with a whisk beater or spoon so as to make the mixture smooth.
Blanch	To heat to boiling water or steam for a short while only to loosen skin, remove colour or set colour.
Blend	To mix two or more ingredients thoroughly.
Bone	To remove bones from meat, poultry, game and fish.
Chill	To place in refrigerator until cold.
Coat	To cover entire surface of food with flour, bread crumbs, or batter.
Cream	To combine butter or other shortening with sugar using a wooden spoon or mixer until light and fluffy.
Croutons	Small cubes of fried bread.
Cut in	To mix butter or margarine with dry ingredients, with pastry blender, knives or fork.
Deep fry	To cook in deep hot fat or oil which covers the food until crisp and golden.

Dice	To cut into small cubes.
Disjoint	To separate the joints of poultry, etc.
Do	To scatter smaller bits of butter or margarine over surface of food.
Flame alcohol;	To spoon alcoholic fluid over food and ignite; to warm the and pour flaming over food.
Fold in	To use a spoon in a gentle rolling circular action as a means of combining ingredients.
Fry	To cook in hot fat using moderate to high heat.
Ghee	Clarified butter, used in curries.
Glaze	A thin coating of beaten egg, milk, syrup or aspic which is brushed over pastry, fruits, ham, chicken, etc.
Grate	To rub food against a grater to form small particles.
Julienne	A term for foods cut into thin strips like matches.
Knead	To work dough with hands until it is of the desired elasticity or consistency.
Marinade	Liquid used for seasoning by soaking usually a mixture of oil, wine and seasonings.
Marinate	To soak in a marinade to soften or add flavour.
Parboil	To boil until partly cooked.
Pate	A highly seasoned meat paste.
Pit	To remove pit-stone or seed from fruit
Poach	To cook gently in simmering liquid.
Pound	To reduce to small particles or a paste, using a pestle and mortar.
Preheat	To turn oven to a selected temperature 10 minutes before it is needed.

Puree	To press through a sieve or put through a food blender to produce a smooth mixture.
Reduce	To cook over a high heat, uncovered, until it is reduced to desired consistency.
Roas	To cook meat by dry heat in oven or on a spit.
Roux	A mixture of fat and flour cooked slowly, stirring frequently - used to thicken sauces, soups, etc.
Salmi	A harh - usually of duck
Saute	To fry lightly in a small amount of fat turning and stirring frequently.
Scald	To pour boiling water over foods.
Score	To cut narrow gashes on the surface of foods.
Shred	To cut into fine strips
Simmer	To cook liquid just below boiling point.
Skin	To remove skin or fat from poultry, etc.
Skim	To remove foam, fat or solid substances from the surface of a cooking mixture.
Sliver	To cut into long thin strips.
Steam	To cook in vapour rising from boiling water.
Stew	A long, slow method of cooking in a liquid in a covered pan, to tenderize tough meats.
Stir	To blend ingredients with a circular motion.
Stock	A liquid containing the flavours, extracts and nutrients of bones, meat, fish or vegetables, in which they are cooked.
Toast	To brown in a toaster or oven.
Toss	To mix lightly, using a fork and a spoon, i.e., salads chiefly.
Whip	To beat rapidly with hand or electric beater or wire whisk.

USEFUL COOKING AND HOUSEHOLD HINTS

1/3 to 1/2 tsp. of dried herbs= 1 Tbsp. fresh herbs.

Rub 1/2 lime on your hands or cutting board to remove onion, garlic or fish odours.

To avoid trouble with weevils, keep flour or cornmeal in a glass jar or plastic container in the refrigerator. 1 Tbsp. oil in water for boiling pasta (macaroni, etc.) prevents it from sticking together.

1 lb. coffee brews 40 cups.

For a tender pie crust use less water than is called for.

Dip knife in hot water to slice hard boiled eggs.

1 cup macaroni makes 2 cups of cooked macaroni.

Freeze left over coffee in an ice cube tray. When used to chill iced coffee, the cubes will not dilute the coffee.

Parsley rinsed in hot water instead of cold retains more flavour.

Brown sugar will not become lumpy if stored in a jar with a piece of blotting paper fitted to the inside of the jar lid.

If food boils over in the oven, cover with salt to prevent smoking and excessive odour.

Add diced crisp bacon and a dash of nutmeg to cauliflower or cabbage for a gourmet touch.

To keep kettles clean, fill with cold water, add some ammonia and bring to a boil. Rinse well.

Gas ovens must be wiped clean before oven is cold. Racks & shelves must be washed with hot water & washing soda.

Wash pewter with hot water and soap, polish will scratch the surface.

Soak tarnished silver in hot water and ammonia - 1 Tbsp. ammonia to quart water.

Mildew stains can be removed by soaking overnight in sour milk; dry in the sun without rinsing. Repeat process if necessary.

To remove a scorch, spread a paste of starch and cold water over the mark. Dry in sun and brush off.

Wash glass windows with crumpled newspaper dipped in cold water, to which has been added a few drops of ammonia.

For wood worms - apply kerosene oil with a brush to the infected area daily for 10 days.

To stop doors creaking rub hinges with soap.

Rust marks can be removed from steel by rubbing with a cut onion.

When washing thermos flasks, add a little vinegar to the water; it removes the musty smell. Do not cork flasks when storing.

To remove stains from china use a rag dipped in cold water and salt.

Before baking have ingredients at room temperature.

To prepare nuts, first blanch; cover with cold water and bring to a boil; let soak until skins wrinkle, then slip the skins off between the fingers.

Parsley freezes well. Cut stems and place bunch in a plastic bag. Thaws easily.

Tear lettuce into pieces instead of cutting to prevent browning.

It is a good idea to make stock from left over bones and keep in the freezer to enhance soups and sauces.

Sour milk can be made by adding 2 tsp. of lime juice to a cup of warm milk, which will curdle it.

Mold should be oiled before it is filled.

Custards baked in hot water should be removed and left to stand for 5 minutes to settle before unmolding. Run knife around the edge; place a plate over the mold, invert the plate and mold, and lift off.

As soon as vegetables are tender drain and plunge into cold water. This sets the colour. Vegetables may be stored and reheated when needed.

Whip cream in a large bowl set in ice. If cream is not available, place a tin of evaporated milk in the freezer for about one hour and then proceed to whip as for cream. To sweeten, use icing sugar, which is preferable to granulated sugar.

OVEN TEMPERATURE GUIDE

	Celsius °C	Fahrenheit °F
Cool	100	200
Very slow	120	250
Slow	150-160	300-325
Moderately slow	160-170	325-350
Moderate	180-190	350-375
Moderate hot	190-200	375-400
Hot	200-230	400-450
Very hot	230-250	450-500

All oven temperatures in this book are in Fahrenheit. Temperatures are meant as a guide - as stoves vary, the manufacturers guide is a good one to follow for your particular stove.

TABLE OF MEASUREMENTS AND MISCELLANEOUS EQUIVALENTS

Dash	Less than 1/8 tsp.
3 tsp.	1 Tbsp.
4 Tbsp.	1/4 cup
8 Tbsp.	1/2 cup
16 Tbsp.	1 cup
1 cup	1/2 pint
2 cups	1 pint
4 cups	1 quart
2 liquid cups	1 lb.
2 pints	1 quart
4 quarts	1 gallon
1 fluid ounce	2 Tbsp.
8 fluid ounces	1 cup
16 ounces	1 pound
1 lb. butter	2 cups
1 carrot	1/2 cup chopped
1/4 lb. cheese	1 cup grated
1 env. gelatin	1 Tbsp.
1 tsp. dried herbs	1 Tbsp. fresh
Juice of Lime	1 Tbsp.
1 medium onion	1/4 cup chopped
1 medium potato	1/2 cup chopped
1 pkg. dry yeast	1/4 oz.

METRIC CONVERSION CHART

METRIC UNITS

1 kilogram (km)	=	1000 grams (gm)
1 gram (gm)	=	1000 milligrams (mg)
1 milligram (mg)	=	1000 micrograms (mcg)

WEIGHTS METRIC   Equivalents

1.0 km	=	1000gm	=	2.2 pounds
0.454 km	=	454gm	=	1.0 pounds
0.100km	=	100gm	=	3.527 ounce
0.028 km	=	28.4gm	=	1.0 ounce

VOLUME LIQUID

4.546 liters	=	4546 ml	=	1 gallon
1.000 liter	=	1000 ml	=	95 quarts
0.946 liter	=	946 ml	=	1 quart
0.473 liter	=	473 ml	=	1 pint
0.015 liter	=	15 ml	=	1 tablespoon
0.005 liter	=	5 ml	=	1 teaspoon

METRIC WEIGHTS

1 cup	=	237 ml	=	8 ounces
1 liter	=	1000 ml	=	1 cubic cm
1 millimeter	=	1 gm		
1 quart	=	946 ml	=	4 cups

Notes

Notes

Printed in Great Britain
by Amazon.co.uk, Ltd.,
Marston Gate.